SENIOR CITIZEN
Coloring Book

Funny Old People Gift for Men and Women

This book belongs to

_____

I'M SORRY I CALLED YOU OLD. I THOUGHT YOU KNEW.

WRINKLED WAS NOT ONE OF THE THINGS I WANTED TO BE WHEN I GREW UP.

YOU KNOW YOU'RE OLD WHEN HAPPY HOUR IS A NAP.

AGE GETS BETTER WITH WINE.

I MAY BE OLD
BUT...WHAT WAS
I SAYING?

BACK IN MY DAY...IF YOU WERE ON THE PHONE YOU COULDN'T LEAVE THE KITCHEN.

I CAME, I SAW, I FORGOT WHAT I WAS DOING. I RETRACED MY STEPS, NOW I HAVE TO PEE.

IT'S WEIRD BEING THE SAME AGE AS OLD PEOPLE.

I'M TOO YOUNG
TO BE THIS OLD!

90's

I STILL THINK 1990 WAS LIKE 10 YEARS AGO.

ALWAYS REMEMBER IT'S BETTER TO WAKE UP AND PEE THAN TO PEE AND WAKE UP.

YOU'RE OLD WHEN YOU REFER TO YOUR KNEES AS GOOD AND BAD INSTEAD OF RIGHT AND LEFT.

INSIDE EVERY OLD PERSON IS A YOUNG ONE WONDERING WHAT THE HELL HAPPENED.

BIRTHDAYS ARE GOOD FOR YOU. STATISTICS SHOW THAT THE PEOPLE WHO HAVE THE MOST LIVE THE LONGEST.

YOU'RE OLD IF YOU USED TO SMOKE CANDY CIGARETTES.

AGE HAS IT'S ADVANTAGES. I JUST CAN'T REMEMBER WHAT THEY ARE.

YOU KNOW YOU'RE OLD WHEN GETTING LUCKY MEANS REMEMBERING WHERE YOU PARKED YOUR CAR.

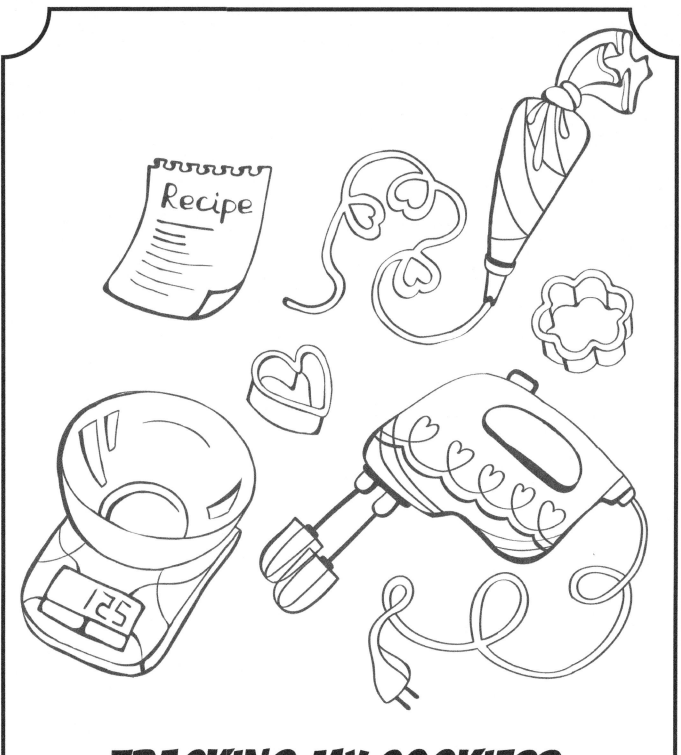

TRACKING MY COOKIES?
THEY'LL NEVER GET MY RECIPES!

YOU'RE OLD WHEN YOU THINK 'I MIGHT AS WELL PEE WHILE I'M HERE' EVERY TIME YOU PASS A BATHROOM.

WHEN YOU'RE OLD AN 'ALL NIGHTER' MEANS NOT GETTING UP TO PEE.

AT LEAST YOU DON'T HAVE TO WORRY ABOUT DYING YOUNG ANYMORE.

YOU'RE OLD WHEN YOUR BACK GOES OUT MORE THAN YOU DO.

YOUNG AT HEART,
JUST OLDER IN
OTHER PLACES.

REMEMBER WHEN YOU COULD GET OUT OF A CHAIR WITHOUT MAKING SOUND EFFECTS?

IF THINGS IMPROVE WITH AGE YOU ARE APPROACHING MAGNIFICANT.

DIDN'T YOU THINK GETTING OLD WOULD TAKE A LITTLE LONGER?

YOU'RE OLD WHEN YOU HAVE GREAT WISDOM TO IMPART BUT YOU JUST CAN'T REMEMBER WHAT IT IS.

DON'T WORRY ABOUT GETTING OLD. YOU'LL STILL DO DUMB STUFF....ONLY SLOWER.

AGE IS AN ISSUE OF MIND OVER MATTER. IF YOU DON'T MIND, IT DOESN'T MATTER.

Printed in Great Britain
by Amazon

26400088R00037